WOMEN &
POWER

MARY BEARD
WOMEN & POWER
A MANIFESTO

P

PROFILE BOOKS

London Review
OF BOOKS

This paperback edition published in 2018

First published in Great Britain in 2017 by
PROFILE BOOKS LTD
3 Holford Yard
Bevin Way
London WC1X 9HD
www.profilebooks.com

and

LONDON REVIEW OF BOOKS
28 Little Russell Street
London WC1A 2HN
www.lrb.co.uk

A version of 'The Public Voice of Women', first appeared in the *London Review of Books*, 20 March 2014; 'Women in Power' was published, also in the *London Review of Books*, 16 March 2017. Both were lectures presented by Mary Beard in the *LRB* Winter Lecture series.

5 7 9 10 8 6 4

Typeset in Elena by MacGuru Ltd
Printed and bound in Great Britain by
CPI Group (UK) Ltd, Croydon CR0 4YY

The moral right of the author has been asserted.

A CIP catalogue record for this book is available from the British Library.

ISBN 978 1 78816 061 2
eISBN 978 1 78283 453 3

For Helen Morales

CONTENTS

PREFACE

WOMEN IN THE WEST have a lot to celebrate; let's not forget. My mother was born before women had the vote in parliamentary elections in Britain. She lived to see a female Prime Minister. Whatever her views of Margaret Thatcher, she was pleased that a woman had reached Number 10 and proud to have had a stake herself in some of those revolutionary changes of the twentieth century. Unlike generations before her, she was able to have a career and marriage and a child (for her own mother pregnancy necessarily meant the end of her job as a teacher). She was a strikingly effective head of a large primary school in the West Midlands. I am sure that she was the very embodiment of *power* to the generations of girls and boys in her charge.

But my mother also knew that it was not all quite so simple, that real equality between women and men was still a thing of the future, and that there were causes for anger as well as for celebration. She always regretted not going to university (and was selflessly pleased that I was able to do just that). She was often frustrated that her views and her voice were not taken as seriously as she hoped they would be. And, though she would have been puzzled at the metaphor of the 'glass ceiling', she was well aware that the further up the career hierarchy she went, the fewer female faces she saw.

She was often in my mind when I was preparing the two lectures on which this book is based, delivered, courtesy of the *London Review of Books*, in 2014 and 2017. I wanted to work out how I would explain to her – as much as to myself, as well as to the millions of other women who still share some of the same frustrations – just how deeply embedded in Western culture are the mechanisms that silence women, that refuse to take them seriously, and that sever them (sometimes quite literally, as we shall see) from the centres of power. This is one place where the world of the ancient Greeks and Romans can help to throw light on our own. When it comes to silencing women, Western culture has had thousands of years of practice.

THE PUBLIC VOICE
OF WOMEN

I WANT TO START very near the beginning of the tradition of Western literature, and its first recorded example of a man telling a woman to 'shut up'; telling her that her voice was not to be heard in public. I am thinking of a moment immortalised at the start of Homer's *Odyssey*, almost 3000 years ago. We tend now to think of the *Odyssey* as the epic story of Odysseus and the adventures and scrapes he had returning home after the Trojan War – while for decades his wife Penelope loyally waited for him, fending off the suitors who were pressing to marry her. But the *Odyssey* is just as much the story of Telemachus, the son of Odysseus and Penelope. It is the story of his growing up and how over the course of the poem he matures from boy to man. That process starts in the first book of the poem when Penelope comes down from her private quarters into the great hall of the palace, to find a bard performing to throngs of her suitors; he is singing about the difficulties the Greek heroes are having in reaching home. She isn't amused, and in front of everyone she asks him to choose another, happier number. At which point young Telemachus intervenes: 'Mother,' he says, 'go back up into your quarters, and take up your own work, the loom and the distaff ... speech will be the business of men, all men, and of me most of all; for mine is the power in this household.' And off she goes, back upstairs.

There is something faintly ridiculous about this wet-behind-the-ears lad shutting up the savvy, middle-aged Penelope. But it is a nice demonstration that right where written evidence for Western culture starts, women's voices are not being heard in the public sphere. More than that, as Homer has it, an integral part of growing up, as a man, is learning to take control of public utterance and to silence the female of the species. The actual words Telemachus uses

1. On this fifth-century BC Athenian pot, Penelope is shown seated by her loom (weaving was always the mark of a good Greek housewife). Telemachus stands in front of her.

are significant too. When he says 'speech' is 'men's business', the word is *muthos* – not in the sense that it has come down to us of 'myth'. In Homeric Greek it signals authoritative public speech, not the kind of chatting, prattling or gossip that anyone – women included, or especially women – could do.

What interests me is the relationship between this classic Homeric moment of silencing a woman and some of the ways in which women's voices are not publicly heard in our own contemporary culture, and in our own politics from the front bench to the shop floor. It is a well-known deafness that's nicely parodied in an old *Punch* cartoon: 'That's an excellent suggestion, Miss Triggs. Perhaps one of the men here would like to make it'. I want to reflect on how it might relate to the abuse that many women who *do* speak out are subjected to even now, and one of the questions at the back of my mind is the connection between publicly speaking out in support of a female logo on a banknote, Twitter threats of rape and

'That's an excellent suggestion, Miss Triggs. Perhaps one of the men here would like to make it.'

2. Almost thirty years ago the cartoonist Riana Duncan captured the sexist atmosphere of the committee or the boardroom. There is hardly a woman who has opened her mouth at a meeting and not had, at some time or other, the 'Miss Triggs treatment'.

decapitation, and Telemachus' put-down of Penelope.

My aim here is to take a long view, a very long view, on the culturally awkward relationship between the voice of women and the public sphere of speech-making, debate and comment: politics in its widest sense, from office committees to the floor of the House. I am hoping that the long view will help us get beyond the simple diagnosis of 'misogyny' that we tend a bit lazily to fall back on. To be sure, 'misogyny' is one way of describing what's going on. (If you go on a television discussion programme and then receive a load of tweets comparing your genitalia to a variety of unpleasantly rotting vegetables, it's hard to find a more apt word.) But if we want to understand – and do something about – the fact that women, even when they are not silenced, still have to pay a very high price for being heard, we need to recognise that it is a bit more complicated and that there is a long back-story.

Telemachus' outburst was just the first

case in a long line of largely successful attempts stretching throughout Greek and Roman antiquity, not only to exclude women from public speech but also to parade that exclusion. In the early fourth century BC, for example, Aristophanes devoted a whole comedy to the 'hilarious' fantasy that women might take over running the state. Part of the joke was that women couldn't speak properly in public – or rather, they couldn't adapt their private speech (which in this case was largely fixated on sex) to the lofty idiom of male politics. In the Roman world, Ovid's *Metamorphoses* – that extraordinary mythological epic about people changing shape (and probably the most influential work of literature on Western art after the Bible) – repeatedly returns to the idea of the silencing of women in the process of their transformation. Poor Io is turned by the god Jupiter into a cow, so she cannot talk but only moo; while the chatty nymph Echo is punished so that her voice is never her own, merely an instrument for

3. David Teniers' seventeenth-century painting shows the moment when Jupiter gives poor Io, now in the shape of a cow, to his wife Juno – to allay any suspicion that his interest in Io might have been inappropriately sexual (which, of course, it was).

repeating the words of others. In Waterhouse's famous painting she gazes at her desired Narcissus but cannot initiate a conversation with him, while he – the original 'narcissist' – has fallen in love with his own image in the pool.

One earnest Roman anthologist of the first century AD was able to rake up just three examples of 'women whose natural condition did not manage to keep them silent in the forum'. His descriptions are revealing. The first, a woman called Maesia, successfully defended herself in the courts and 'because she really had a man's nature behind the appearance of a woman was called the "androgyne"'. The second, Afrania, used to initiate legal cases herself and was 'impudent' enough to plead in person, so that everyone became tired out with her 'barking' or 'yapping' (she still isn't allowed human 'speech'). We are told that she died in 48 BC, because 'with unnatural freaks like this it's more important to record when they died than when they were born.'

4. In John William Waterhouse's striking dreamy version of the scene (painted in 1903), the semi-clad Echo gazes speechless at her 'narcissist' preoccupied with his own image in the pool.

There are only two main exceptions in the classical world to this abomination of women's public speaking. First, women are allowed to speak out as victims and as martyrs, usually to preface their own death. Early Christian women were represented loudly upholding their faith as they went to the lions; and, in a well-known story from the early history of Rome, the virtuous Lucretia, raped by a brutal prince of the ruling monarchy, was given a speaking part solely to denounce the rapist and announce her own suicide (or so Roman writers presented it: what really happened, we haven't a clue). But even this rather bitter opportunity to speak could itself be removed. One story in the *Metamorphoses* tells of the rape of the young princess Philomela. In order to prevent any Lucretia-style denunciation, the rapist quite simply cuts her tongue out. It's a notion that's picked up in Shakespeare's *Titus Andronicus*, where the tongue of the raped Lavinia is also ripped out.

The second exception is more familiar.

5. This sixteenth-century manuscript gives the two key episodes of Lucretia's story. On the upper register, Sextus Tarquinius attacks the virtuous woman (his clothes are disconcertingly neatly laid out beside the bed); on the lower, Lucretia in sixteenth-century dress denounces the rapist to her family.

6. *Picasso's version, from 1930, of Tereus' rape of Philomela.*

Occasionally women could legitimately rise up to speak – to defend their homes, their children, their husbands or the interests of other women. So in the third of the three examples of female oratory discussed by that Roman anthologist, the woman, Hortensia by name, gets away with it because she is acting explicitly as the spokesperson for the women of Rome (and for women only), after they have been subject to a special wealth tax to fund a dubious war effort. Women, in other words, may in extreme circumstances publicly defend their own sectional interests, but not speak for men or the community as a whole. In general, as one second-century AD guru put it, 'a woman should as modestly guard against exposing her voice to outsiders as she would guard against stripping off her clothes.'

There is more to all this than meets the eye, however. This 'muteness' is not just a reflection of women's general disempowerment throughout the classical world: no voting rights, limited legal and economic independence and so on. It was partly that. Ancient women were obviously not likely to raise their voices in a political sphere in which they had no formal stake. But we are dealing with a much more active and loaded exclusion of women from public speech – and one with a much greater impact than we usually acknowledge on our own traditions, conventions and assumptions about the voice of women. What I mean is that public speaking and oratory were not merely things that ancient women *didn't do*: they were exclusive practices and skills that defined masculinity as a gender. As we saw with Telemachus, to become a man (or at least an elite man) was to claim the right to speak. Public speech was a – if not *the* – defining attribute of maleness. Or, to quote a well-known Roman slogan, the elite male citizen could be summed up as *vir bonus dicendi peritus*, 'a good man, skilled in speaking'. A woman speaking in public was, in most circumstances, by definition not a woman.

·cx·

HORTENSIA

zpten/ als der römer regierung vñ drp man gesetzt
was /dz durch die selben / in ainer noc den gemainen

7. Hortensia features in Boccaccio's *compendium* of Famous
Women. *In this late fifteenth-century edition, she is pictured
very much in fifteenth-century guise boldly leading her posse
of female followers to confront the Roman authorities.*

We find repeated stress throughout ancient literature on the authority of the deep male voice in contrast to the female. As one ancient scientific treatise explicitly put it, a low-pitched voice indicated manly courage, a high-pitched voice female cowardice. Other classical writers insisted that the tone and timbre of women's speech always threatened to subvert not just the voice of the male orator but also the social and political stability, the health, of the whole state. One second-century AD lecturer and intellectual with the revealing name of Dio Chrysostom (it means literally Dio 'the Golden Mouth') asked his audience to imagine a situation where 'an entire community was struck by the following strange affliction: all the men suddenly got female voices, and no male – child or adult – could say anything in a manly way. Would not that seem terrible and harder to bear than any plague? I'm sure they would send off to a sanctuary to consult the gods and try to propitiate the divine power with many gifts.' He wasn't joking.

This is not the peculiar ideology of some distant culture. Distant in time it may be. But I want to underline that this is a tradition of gendered speaking – and the theorising of gendered speaking – to which we are still, directly or more often indirectly, the heirs. Let's not overstate the case. Western culture does not owe everything to the Greeks and Romans, in speaking or in anything else (thank heavens it doesn't; none of us would fancy living in a Greco-Roman world). There are all kinds of variant and competing influences on us, and our political system has happily overthrown many of the gendered certainties of antiquity. Yet it remains the fact that our own traditions of debate and public speaking, their conventions and rules, still lie very much in the shadow of the classical world. The modern techniques of rhetoric and persuasion formulated in the Renaissance were drawn explicitly from ancient speeches and handbooks. Our own terms of rhetorical analysis go back directly to Aristotle and Cicero (before the era of

Donald Trump it used to be common to point out that Barack Obama, or his speech writers, had learned their best tricks from Cicero). And those nineteenth-century gentlemen who devised, or enshrined, most of the parliamentary rules and procedures in the House of Commons were brought up on exactly those classical theories, slogans and prejudices that I have been quoting. Again, we're not simply the victims or dupes of our classical inheritance but classical traditions have provided us with a powerful template for thinking about public speech, and for deciding what counts as good oratory or bad, persuasive or not, and whose speech is to be given space to be heard. And gender is obviously an important part of that mix.

IT TAKES ONLY A CASUAL glance at the modern Western traditions of speech-making – at least up to the twentieth century – to see that many of the classical themes I have been highlighting emerge time and time again. Women who claim a public voice get treated as freakish androgynes, like Maesia who defended herself in the Forum – or they apparently treat themselves as such. The obvious case is Elizabeth I's belligerent address to the troops at Tilbury in 1588 in the face of the Spanish Armada. In the words many of us learned at school, she seems positively to avow her own androgyny:

> I know I have the body of a weak, feeble woman; but I have the heart and stomach of a king, and of a king of England too

– an odd slogan to get young girls to learn. The truth is that she probably never said anything of the sort. There is no script from her hand or that of her speech-writer, no eyewitness account, and the canonical version comes from the letter of an unreliable commentator, with his own axe to grind, written almost forty years later. But for my purpose the probable fictionality of the speech makes

8. An image of Queen Elizabeth at Tilbury often reproduced in nineteenth-century British school textbooks. The Queen in her delicate, fly-away dress is entirely surrounded by men – and pikes.

it even better: the nice twist is that the male letter-writer puts the boast (or confession) of androgyny into Elizabeth's own mouth.

Looking at modern traditions of oratory more generally, we also find the same areas of licence for women to talk publicly, whether in support of their own sectional interests, or to parade their victimhood. If you search out the women's contributions included in those curious compendia, called 'one hundred great speeches in history' and the like, you'll find that most of the female highlights from Emmeline Pankhurst to Hillary Clinton's address to the UN conference on women in Beijing are about the lot of women. So too is probably the most popularly anthologised example of female oratory of all, the 1851 'Ain't I a Woman?' speech of Sojourner Truth, ex-slave, abolitionist and American campaigner for women's rights. 'And ain't I a woman?' she is supposed to have said.

I have borne 13 chilern, and seen 'em mos'

all sold off to slavery, and when I cried out with my mother's grief, none but Jesus heard me! And ain't I a woman ...

I should say that influential as these words have been, they are only slightly less mythical than Elizabeth's at Tilbury. The authorised version was written up a decade or so after Sojourner Truth said whatever she said. That is when the now famous refrain, which she certainly did not say, was inserted, while at the same time her words as a whole were translated into a Southern drawl, to match the abolitionist message – even though she came from the North and had been brought up speaking Dutch. I'm not saying that women's voices raised in support of women's causes were not, or are not, important (*someone* has to speak up for women); but it remains the case that women's public speech has for centuries been 'niched' into that area.

Even that licence has not always or consistently been available to women. There

9. *Photographed in 1870, when she was over seventy,*
Sojourner Truth is here made to look anything but radical
– instead, a rather sedately venerable old lady.

are countless examples of attempts to write women entirely out of public discourse, Telemachus-style. A notorious recent case was the silencing of Elizabeth Warren in the US Senate – and her exclusion from the debate – when she attempted to read out a letter by Coretta Scott King. Few of us, I suspect, know enough about the rules of senatorial debate to know how justified this was, formally. But those rules did not stop Bernie Sanders and other senators (admittedly in her support) reading out exactly the same letter and *not* being excluded. But there are unsettling literary examples too.

One of the main themes of Henry James' *Bostonians*, published in the 1880s, is the silencing of Verena Tarrant, a young feminist campaigner and speaker. As she draws closer to her suitor Basil Ransom (a man endowed, as James stresses, with a rich deep voice), she finds herself increasingly unable to speak, as she once did, in public. Ransom effectively re-privatises her voice, insisting that she speak only to him: 'Keep your soothing words for me,' he says. In the novel James' own standpoint is hard to pin down – certainly readers have not warmed to Ransom – but in his essays James makes it clear where he stood; for he wrote about the polluting, contagious and socially destructive effect of women's voices, in words that could easily have come from the pen of some second-century AD Roman (and were almost certainly in part derived from classical sources). Under American women's influence, he insisted, language risks becoming a 'generalised mumble or jumble, a tongueless slobber or snarl or whine'; it will sound like 'the moo of the cow, the bray of the ass, and the bark of the dog'. (Note the echo of the tongueless Philomela, the moo of Io, and the barking of the female orator in the Roman Forum.) James was one among many. In what amounted to a crusade at the time for proper standards in American speech, other prominent contemporaries praised the sweet domestic singing of the female voice, while entirely opposing its use in the wider world. And there was plenty of thundering about the 'thin nasal tones' of women's public speech, about their 'twangs, whiffles, snuffles, whines and whinnies'. 'In the names of our homes, our children, of our future, our national honour,' James said again, 'don't let us have women like that!'

Of course, we don't talk in those bald terms now. Or not quite. For many aspects of this traditional package of views about the unsuitability of women for public speaking in general – a package going back in its essentials over two millennia – still underlie some of our own assumptions about, and awkwardness with, the female voice in public. Take the language we still use to describe the sound of women's speech, which is not all that far from James or those pontificating Romans. In making a public case, in fighting their corner, in speaking out, what are women said to be? 'Strident'; they 'whinge' and they 'whine'. After one particular vile bout of internet comments on my own genitalia, I tweeted (rather pluckily,

I thought) that it was all a bit 'gob-smack-ing'. This was reported by one commentator in a mainstream British magazine in these terms: 'The misogyny is truly "gob-smack-ing", she *whined*.' (So far as I can see from a quick Google trawl, the only other group in this country said to 'whine' as much as women are unpopular Premiership football managers on a losing streak.)

Do those words matter? Of course they do, because they underpin an idiom that acts to remove the authority, the force, even the humour from what women have to say. It is an idiom that effectively repositions women back into the domestic sphere (people 'whinge' over things like the washing up); it trivialises their words, or it 're-privatises' them. Contrast the 'deep-voiced' man with all the connotations of profundity that the simple word 'deep' brings. It is still the case that when listeners hear a female voice, they do not hear a voice that connotes authority; or rather they have not learned how to hear authority in it; they don't hear *muthos*. And it is not just voice: you can add in the craggy or wrinkled faces that signal mature wisdom in the case of a bloke, but 'past-my-use-by-date' in the case of a woman.

They do not tend to hear a voice of expertise either; at least, not outside the traditional spheres of women's sectional interests. For a female MP to be Minister of Women (or of Education or Health) is a very different thing from being Chancellor of the Exchequer, a post which no woman in the United Kingdom has yet filled. And, across the board, we still see tremendous resistance to female encroachment onto traditional male discursive territory, whether it's the abuse hurled at Jacqui Oatley for having the nerve to stray from the netball court to become the first woman commentator on *Match of the Day*, or what can be meted out to women who appear on *Question Time*, where the range of topics discussed is usually fairly mainstream 'male political'. It may not be a surprise that the same commentator who accused me of 'whining' claims to run a

10. Jacqui Oatley receives an honorary degree in 2016. When she started as commentator on Match of the Day in 2007, there was an explosion of criticism. 'An insult to the controlled commentaries' of men, one said; 'I'll be changing channels' said another.

'small, light-hearted' competition for the 'most stupid woman to appear on *Question Time*'. More interesting is another cultural connection this reveals: that unpopular, controversial or just plain different views when voiced by a woman are taken as indications of her stupidity. It is not that you disagree, it is that *she* is stupid: 'Sorry, love, you just don't understand.' I've lost count of the number of times I've been called 'an ignorant moron'.

These attitudes, assumptions and prejudices are hard-wired into us: not into our brains (there is no neurological reason for us to hear low-pitched voices as more authoritative than high-pitched ones), but into our culture, our language and millennia of our history. And when we are thinking about the under-representation of women in national politics, their relative muteness in the public sphere, we have to think beyond what some prominent British politicians and their chums got up to in the Oxford Bullingdon Club, beyond the bad behaviour and blokeish culture of Westminster, beyond even family-friendly hours and childcare provision (important as those are). We have to focus on the even more fundamental issues of how we have learned to hear the contributions of women or – going back to that *Punch* cartoon for a moment – on what I'd like to call the 'Miss Triggs question'. Not just, how does she get a word in edgeways? But how can we make ourselves more aware about the processes and prejudices that make us not listen to her.

SOME OF THESE SAME issues of voice and gender are at play in the questions of internet trolls, and the hostility – from abuse to death threats – that get transmitted online. We have to be careful about generalising too confidently about the nastier sides of the internet. They appear in many different forms (it's not quite the same on Twitter, for example, as it is under the line in a newspaper comment section) and criminal death threats are a different kettle of fish from merely 'unpleasant' sexist abuse. People of all sorts are the targets, from grieving parents of dead teenagers to 'celebrities' of many kinds. What is clear – though precise estimates vary – is that many more men than women are the perpetrators of this stuff, and they attack women far more than they attack men. For what it's worth (and I have not suffered anything like as much as some women), I receive something we might euphemistically call an 'inappropriately hostile' response – that is to say, more than fair criticism or even fair anger – every time I speak on radio or television.

This abuse is driven, I am sure, by many different things. Some of it is from kids acting up; some from people who've had far too much to drink; some from people who for a moment have lost their inner inhibitors (and can be very apologetic later). More are sad than are villainous. When I'm feeling charitable I think quite a lot comes from people who feel let down by the false promises of democratisation blazoned by, for example, Twitter. It was supposed to put us directly in touch with those in power, and open up a new democratic kind of conversation. It does almost nothing of the sort: if we tweet the prime minister or the Pope, they no more read our words than if we send them a letter – and for the most part, the prime minister does not even write the tweets that appear under her or his name. How could she? (I'm not so sure about the Pope.) Some of the abuse, I suspect, is a squeal of frustration at those false promises, taking aim at a convenient traditional target ('a gobby woman'). Women, let's remember, are not the only ones who may feel themselves 'voiceless'.

But the more I have looked at the threats and insults that women have received, the more they seem to fit into the old patterns that I have been talking about. For a start it doesn't much matter what line you take as a woman, if you venture into traditional male territory, the abuse comes anyway. It is not *what* you say that prompts it, it's simply the fact that you're saying it. And that matches the detail of the threats themselves. They include a fairly predictable menu of rape, bombing, murder and so forth (this may sound very relaxed; that doesn't mean it's not scary when it comes late at night). But a significant subsection is directed at silencing the woman. 'Shut up you bitch' is a fairly common refrain. Or it promises to remove the capacity of the woman to speak. 'I'm going to cut off your head and rape it' was one tweet I got. 'Headlessfemalepig' was the Twitter name chosen by someone threatening an American journalist. 'You should have your tongue ripped out' was tweeted to another woman.

In its crude, aggressive way, this is about keeping, or getting, women out of man's talk. It is hard not to see some faint connection between these mad Twitter outbursts – most of them are just that – and the men in the House of Commons heckling women MPs so loudly that you simply cannot hear what they're saying. (In the Afghan parliament, apparently, they disconnect the mics when they don't want to hear the women speak). Ironically, the well-meaning solution often recommended when women are on the receiving end of this stuff turns out to bring about the very result the abusers want: namely, their silence. 'Don't call the abusers out. Don't give them any attention; that's what they want. Just keep mum and "block" them' you're told. It is an uncanny reprise of the old advice to women of 'put up and shut up', and it risks leaving the bullies in unchallenged occupation of the playground.

So much for the diagnosis: what's the practical remedy? Like most women, I wish I knew. There can't be a group of female friends or colleagues anywhere, which hasn't regularly discussed the day-to-day aspects of the 'Miss Triggs question', whether in the office, or a committee room, council chamber, seminar or the House of Commons. How do I get my point heard? How do I get it noticed? How do I get to belong in the discussion? I am sure it is something some men feel too, but if there's one thing that bonds women of all backgrounds, of all political colours, in all kinds of business and profession, it is the classic experience of the failed intervention; you're at a meeting, you make a point, then a short silence follows, and after a few awkward seconds some man picks up where he had just left off: 'What I was saying was ...' You might as well never have opened your mouth, and you end up blaming both yourself and the men whose exclusive club the discussion appears to be.

Those who do manage successfully to get their voice across very often adopt some version of the 'androgyne' route, like Maesia in the Forum or 'Elizabeth' at Tilbury, consciously aping aspects of male rhetoric. That was what Margaret Thatcher did when she took voice training specifically to lower her voice, to add the tone of authority that her advisers thought her high pitch lacked. If that worked, it is perhaps churlish to knock it. But all tactics of that type tend to leave

women still feeling on the outside, imper-
sonators of rhetorical roles that they don't
feel they own. Putting it bluntly, having
women pretend to be men may be a quick
fix, but it doesn't get to the heart of the
problem.

We need to think more fundamentally
about the rules of our rhetorical operations.
I don't mean the old stand-by of 'men and
women talk different languages, after all' (if
they do, it's surely because they have been
taught different languages). And I certainly
don't mean to suggest that we go down
the 'Men are from Mars, Women are from
Venus' route of pop-psychology. My hunch
is that if we are going to make real progress
with the 'Miss Triggs question', we need to
go back to some first principles about the
nature of spoken authority, about what
constitutes it, and how we have learned to
hear authority where we do. And rather than
push women into voice training classes to
get a nice, deep, husky and entirely artificial
tone, we should be thinking more about the

fault-lines and fractures that underlie dominant male discourse.

Here again we can usefully look to the Greeks and Romans. For, while it is true that classical culture is partly responsible for our starkly gendered assumptions about public speech, male *muthos* and female silence, it is also the case that some ancient writers were much more reflective than we are about those assumptions: they were subversively aware of what was at stake in them, they were troubled by their simplicity, and they hinted at resistance. Ovid may have emphatically silenced his women in their transformation or mutilation, but he also suggested that communication could transcend the human voice, and that women were not that easily silenced. Philomela lost her tongue, but she still managed to denounce her rapist by weaving the story into a tapestry (which is why Shakespeare's Lavinia has her hands, as well as her tongue, removed). The smartest ancient rhetorical theorists were prepared to acknowledge

11. In Edward Burne-Jones' strikingly 'medieval' version of the scene, from 1896, the voiceless Philomela is depicted as having woven the story of her rape into the fabric of the cloth behind her.

that the best male techniques of oratorical persuasion were uncomfortably close to the techniques (as they saw it) of female seduction. Was oratory then really so safely masculine, they worried.

One particularly bloody anecdote vividly exposes the unresolved gender wars that lay just below the surface of ancient public life and speaking. In the course of the Roman civil wars that followed the assassination of Julius Caesar in 44 BC, Marcus Tullius Cicero – the most powerful public speaker and debater in the Roman world, ever – was lynched. The hit-squad that took him out triumphantly brought his head and hands to Rome, and pinned them up, for all to see, on the speaker's platform in the Forum. It was then, so the story went, that Fulvia, the wife of Mark Antony, who had been the victim of some of Cicero's most devastating polemics, went along to have a look. And when she saw those bits of him, she removed the pins from her hair and repeatedly stabbed them into the dead man's tongue. It's a disconcerting image

12. In the 1880s Pavel Svedomsky offered an unnervingly erotic version of Fulvia gloating over the head of Cicero – which she appears to have taken back home.

of one of the defining articles of female adorn-
ment, the hairpin, used as a weapon against
the very site of the production of male speech
– a kind of reverse Philomela.

What I am pointing to here is a critically
self-aware ancient tradition: not one that
directly challenges the basic template I have
been outlining, but one that is determined
to reveal its conflicts and paradoxes, and
to raise bigger questions about the nature
and purpose of speech, male or female. We
should perhaps take our cue from this, and
try to bring to the surface the kinds of question we tend to shelve about how we speak
in public, why and whose voice fits. What we
need is some old fashioned consciousness-
raising about what we mean by the 'voice
of authority' and how we've come to con-
struct it. We need to work that out before we
figure out how we modern Penelopes might
answer back to our own Telemachuses –
or, for that matter, just decide to lend Miss
Triggs some hairpins.

WOMEN IN POWER

IN 1915 CHARLOTTE PERKINS GILMAN published a funny, but unsettling, story entitled *Herland*. As the name hints, it is a fantasy about a nation of women – and women only – that has existed for 2,000 years in some remote, still unexplored part of the globe. These women live in a magnificent utopia: clean and tidy, collaborative, peaceful – even the cats have stopped killing the birds – brilliantly organised in everything from its sustainable agriculture and delicious food to its social services and education. And it all depends on one miraculous innovation. At the very beginning of its history, the founding mothers had somehow perfected the technique of parthenogenesis. The practical details are a bit unclear, but the women somehow just gave birth to baby girls, with no intervention from men at all. There was no sex in Herland.

HERLAND

Charlotte Perkins Stetson Gilman

13. This cover of Herland captures the strange Utopian
fantasy of Gilman's novel – not without its elements
of early twentieth-century racism and eugenics.

The story is all about the disruption of this world when three American males discover it: Vandyck Jennings, the nice-guy narrator; Jeff Margrave, a man whose gallantry is almost the undoing of him in the face of all these ladies; and the truly appalling Terry Nicholson. When they first arrive, Terry refuses to believe that there are not some men around somewhere, pulling the strings, because how, after all, could you imagine women actually running anything? When eventually he has to accept that this is exactly what they are doing, he decides that what Herland needs is a bit of sex and a bit of male mastery. The story ends with Terry unceremoniously deported after one of his bids for mastery, in the bedroom, goes horribly wrong.

There are all kinds of irony to this tale. One joke that Perkins Gilman plays throughout is that the women simply don't recognise their own achievements. They have independently created an exemplary state, one to be proud of, but when confronted by their three uninvited male visitors, who lie some-where on the spectrum between spineless and scumbag, they tend to defer to the men's competence, knowledge and expertise; and they are slightly in awe of the male world outside. Although they have made a utopia, they think they have messed it all up.

But *Herland* points to bigger questions, about how we recognise female power, and about the sometimes funny, sometimes frightening stories we tell ourselves about it – and indeed have told ourselves about it, in the West at least, for thousands of years. How have we learned to look at those women who exercise power, or who try to? What are the cultural underpinnings of misogyny in politics or the workplace, and its forms (what kind of misogyny, aimed at what or whom, using what words or images, and with what effects)? How and why do the conventional definitions of 'power' (or for that matter of 'knowledge', 'expertise' and 'authority') that we carry round in our heads exclude women?

It is happily the case that there are now more women in what we would all probably agree are 'powerful' positions than there were ten, let alone fifty years ago. Whether that is as politicians, councillors, police commissioners, managers, CEOs, judges or whatever, it is still a clear minority – but there are *more*. (To give just one figure, around 4 per cent of UK MPs were women in the 1970s; around 30 per cent are now.) But my basic premise is that our mental, cultural template for a powerful person remains resolutely male. If we close our eyes and try to conjure up the image of a president or – to move into the knowledge economy – a professor, what most of us see is not a woman. And that is just as true even if you *are* a woman professor: the cultural stereotype is so strong that, at the level of those close-your-eyes fantasies, it is still hard for *me* to imagine *me*, or someone like me, in my role. I put the phrase 'cartoon professor' into Google UK Images: 'cartoon professor' to make sure that I was targeting the imaginary ones, the cultural template, not the real ones; and 'UK' to exclude the slightly different definition of 'professor' in the USA. Out of the first hundred that came up, only one, Professor Holly from Pokémon Farm, was female.

To put this the other way round, we have no template for what a powerful woman looks like, except that she looks rather like a man. The regulation trouser suits, or at least the trousers, worn by so many Western female political leaders, from Angela Merkel to Hillary Clinton, may be convenient and practical; they may be a signal of the refusal to become a clothes horse, which is the fate of so many political wives; but they are also a simple tactic – like lowering the timbre of the voice – to make the female appear more male, to fit the part of power. Elizabeth I (or whoever invented her famous speech) knew exactly what the game was when she said she had 'the heart and stomach of a king'. And it was that idea of the divorce between women and power that made Melissa

14. Angela Merkel and Hillary Clinton spotted together in their female politicians' uniform.

McCarthy's parodies of the one time White House press secretary Sean Spicer on *Saturday Night Live* so effective. It was said that these annoyed President Trump more than most satires on his regime, because, according to one of the 'sources close to him', 'he doesn't like his people to appear weak.' Decode that, and what it actually means is that he doesn't like his men to be parodied by and as women. Weakness comes with a female gender.

It follows from this that women are still perceived as belonging outside power. We may sincerely want them to get to the inside of it or we may, by various often unconscious means, cast women as interlopers when they make it. (I still remember a Cambridge where, in most colleges, the women's loos were tucked away across two courts, through the passage and down the stairs in the basement: is there a message here, I wondered.) But, in every way, the shared metaphors we use of female access to power – 'knocking on the door', 'storming the citadel', 'smashing the glass ceiling', or just giving them a 'leg up' – underline female exteriority. Women in power are seen as breaking down barriers, or alternatively as taking something to which they are not quite entitled.

A headline in *The Times* in early 2017 captured this wonderfully. Above an article reporting on the possibility that women might soon gain the positions of Metropolitan Police commissioner, chair of the BBC Unitary Board and bishop of London, it read: 'Women Prepare for a Power Grab in Church, Police and BBC.' (Cressida Dick, the commissioner of the Met, was the only one of these predictions to come true.) Of course, headline writers are paid to 'grab' attention. But even so, the idea that you could present the prospect of a woman becoming bishop of London as a '*power grab*' – and that probably thousands upon thousands of readers didn't bat an eyelid when they read it – is a sure sign that we need to look a lot more carefully at our cultural assumptions about women's relationship with power. Workplace nurseries, family-friendly hours, mentoring schemes and all those practical things are importantly enabling, but they are only part of what we need to be doing. If we want to give women as a gender – and not just in the shape of a few determined individuals – their place inside of the structures of power, we have to think harder about how and why we think as we do. If there is a cultural template, which works to disempower women, what exactly is it and where do we get it from?

At this point, it may be useful to start thinking about the classical world. More often than we may realise, and in sometimes quite shocking ways, we are still using ancient Greek idioms to represent the idea of women in, and out of, power. There is at first sight an impressive array of powerful female characters in the repertoire of Greek myth and storytelling. In real life, ancient women had no formal political rights, and precious little economic or social independence; in some cities, such as

Athens, 'respectable', elite married women were rarely seen outside the home. But Athenian drama in particular, and the Greek imagination more generally, has offered *our* imaginations a series of unforgettable women: Medea, Clytemnestra and Antigone among many others.

They are not, however, role models – far from it. For the most part, they are portrayed as abusers rather than users of power. They take it illegitimately, in a way that leads to chaos, to the fracture of the state, to death and destruction. They are monstrous hybrids, who are not, in the Greek sense, women at all. And the unflinching logic of their stories is that they must be disempowered and put back in their place. In fact, it is the unquestionable mess that women make of power in Greek myth that justifies their exclusion from it in real life, and justifies the rule of men. (I can't help thinking that Perkins Gilman was lightly parodying this logic when she made the women of Herland believe that they had messed up.)

Go back to one of the very earliest Greek dramas to survive, the *Agamemnon* of Aeschylus, first performed in 458 BC, and you'll find that its antiheroine, Clytemnestra, horribly encapsulates that ideology. In the play, she becomes the effective ruler of her city while her husband is away fighting the Trojan War; and in the process she ceases to be a woman. Aeschylus repeatedly uses male terms and the language of masculinity to refer to her. In the very first lines, for example, her character is described as *androboulon* – a hard word to translate neatly but something like 'with manly purpose', or 'thinking like a man'. And, of course, the power that Clytemnestra illegitimately claims is put to destructive purpose when she murders Agamemnon in his bath on his return. The patriarchal order is only restored when Clytemnestra's children conspire to kill her.

There's a similar logic in the stories of that mythical race of Amazon women, said by Greek writers to exist somewhere

15. Frederic Leighton's late nineteenth-century statuesque version of Clytemnestra also gestures to her masculine side, in the heavy arms and unisex outfit.

on the northern borders of their world. A more violent and more militaristic lot than the peaceful denizens of Herland, this monstrous regiment always threatened to overrun the civilised world of Greece and Greek men. An enormous amount of modern feminist energy has been wasted on trying to prove that these Amazons did once exist, with all the seductive possibilities of a historical society that really was ruled by and for women. Dream on. The hard truth is that the Amazons were a Greek male myth. The basic message was that the only good Amazon was a dead one, or – to go back to awful Terry – one that had been mastered, in the bedroom. The underlying point was that it was the duty of men to save civilisation from the rule of women.

There are, it is true, occasional examples where it might look as if we are getting a more positive version of ancient female power. One staple of the modern stage is Aristophanes' comedy known by the name of its lead female character, *Lysistrata*.

16. *The conflict between Amazons and Greeks decorates a fifth-century* BC *Athenian pot. The Amazons here wear the ancient equivalent of patterned 'onesies', or nifty tunics and leggings. For an ancient viewer, this style of dress would signal those real-life enemies of the Greeks: the Persians.*

17. *Love at last sight. On this sixth-century BC Athenian pot, the Greek hero Achilles kills Penthesilea, the Amazon Queen – as he spears her, they fall in love. Too late.*

Written in the late fifth century BC, it is still a popular choice because it appears to be a perfect mixture of highbrow classics, feisty feminism, a stop-the-war agenda and a good sprinkling of smut (and it was once translated by Germaine Greer). It's the story of a sex-strike, set not in the world of myth but in the contemporary world of ancient Athens. Under Lysistrata's leadership, the women try to force their husbands to end the long-running war with Sparta by refusing to sleep with them until they do. The men go round for most of the play with enormously inconvenient erections (which now tends to cause some difficulty and hilarity in the costume department). Eventually, unable to bear their encumbrances any longer, they give in to the women's demands and make peace. Girl power at its finest, you might think. Athena, the patron deity of the city, is often wheeled out on the positive side too. Doesn't the simple fact that she was female suggest a more nuanced version of the imagined sphere of women's influence?

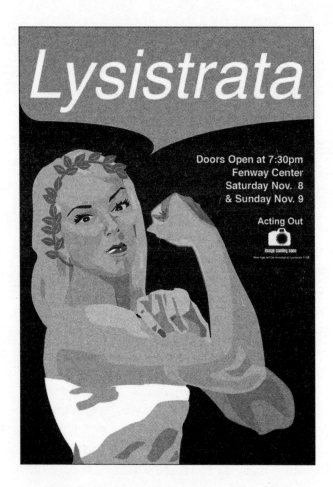

18. In this poster for a 2015 production of Lysistrata, the famous image of 'Rosie the Riveter' is combined with a classical Greek woman – to give a feminist punch.

19. *The erections of the sex-starved men in Lysistrata often present a problem for modern productions. Here is a solution from a recent production: the elongated squeezy bottle.*

I am afraid not. If you scratch the surface and go back to the fifth-century context, *Lysistrata* looks very different. It is not just that the original audience and actors consisted, according to Athenian convention, entirely of men – the female characters were probably played much like pantomime dames. It is also the fact that, at the end, the fantasy of women's power is firmly stamped down. In the final scene, the peace process consists of bringing a naked woman onto the stage (or a man somehow dressed up as a naked woman), who is used as if she were a map of Greece, and is metaphorically carved up in an uncomfortably pornographic way between the men of Athens and Sparta. Not much proto-feminism there.

As for Athena, it is true that in those binary charts of ancient Greek gods and goddesses that appear in modern textbooks ('Zeus, king of the gods; Hera, wife of Zeus'), she appears on the female side. But the crucial thing about her in the ancient context is that she is another of those difficult hybrids. In

20. This Roman miniature copy of the statue of the goddess Athena in the Parthenon captures her male aspects, from the shield and breastplate to the image of (military) victory in her hand. In the centre of her breastplate is the head of Medusa.

the Greek sense she is not a woman at all. For a start she's dressed as a warrior, when fighting was exclusively male work (that's an underlying problem with the Amazons too, of course). Then she's a virgin, when the raison d'être of the female sex was breeding new citizens. And she herself wasn't even born of a mother but directly from the head of her father, Zeus. It was almost as if Athena, woman or not, offered a glimpse of an ideal male world in which women could not only be kept in their place but dispensed with entirely.

The point is simple but important: as far back as we can see in Western history there is a radical separation – real, cultural and imaginary – between women and power. But there is one item of Athena's costume that brings this right up to our own day. On most images of the goddess, at the very centre of her body armour, fixed onto her breastplate, is the image of a female head, with writhing snakes for hair. This is the head of Medusa, one of three mythical sisters known as the

Gorgons, and it was one of the most potent ancient symbols of male mastery over the destructive dangers that the very possibility of female power represented. It is no accident that we find her decapitated – her head proudly paraded as an accessory by this decidedly un-female female deity.

There are many ancient variations on Medusa's story. One famous version has her as a beautiful woman raped by Poseidon in a temple of Athena, who promptly transformed her, as punishment for the sacrilege (punishment to *her*, note), into a monstrous creature with a deadly capacity to turn to stone anyone who looked at her face. It later became the task of the hero Perseus to kill this woman, and he cut her head off using his shiny shield as a mirror so as to avoid having to look directly at her. At first he used the head as a weapon since even in death it retained the capacity to petrify. He then presented it to Athena, who displayed it on her own armour (one message being: take care not to look too directly at the goddess).

21. *In a fantastical form of childbirth, on this sixth-century* BC *Athenian pot Athena is shown being born directly from the head of Zeus, while other gods and goddesses look on. The apparent madness of Greek myth has an important and awkward point here: in a perfect world you would not even need women to procreate.*

It hardly needs Freud to see those snaky locks as an implied claim to phallic power. This is the classic myth in which the dominance of the male is violently reasserted against the illegitimate power of the woman. And Western literature, culture and art have repeatedly returned to it in those terms. The bleeding head of Medusa is a familiar sight among our own modern masterpieces, often loaded with questions about the power of the artist to represent an object at which no one should look. In 1598 Caravaggio did an extraordinary version of the decapitated head with his own features, so it is said, screaming in horror, blood pouring out, the snakes still writhing. A few decades earlier Benvenuto Cellini made a large bronze statue of Perseus which still stands in the Piazza della Signoria in Florence: the hero is depicted trampling on the mangled corpse of Medusa, and holding her head up in the air, again with the blood and the gunge pouring out of it.

What is extraordinary is that this

22. Heroic triumphalism or sadistic misogyny? In Benvenuto
Cellini's statue, Perseus holds up the severed head of
Medusa, while he tramples on her dead body. It makes
an apt pair with the sculpture just behind it: the Greek
hero Achilles violently abducting a Trojan princess.

beheading remains even now a cultural symbol of opposition to women's power. Angela Merkel's features have again and again been superimposed on Caravaggio's image. In one of the sillier outbursts in this vein, a column in the magazine of the Police Federation once, during her time as home secretary, dubbed Theresa May the 'Medusa of Maidenhead'. 'The Medusa comparison might be a bit strong,' the *Daily Express* responded: 'We all know that Mrs May has beautifully coiffed hair.' And one cartoon circulating at the 2017 Labour party conference featured an image of 'Maydusa', snakes and all. May got off lightly, though, compared with Dilma Rousseff, who drew a very short straw indeed when she was President of Brazil and had to open a major Caravaggio show in São Paolo. The *Medusa* was naturally in it, and Rousseff standing in front of the very painting proved an irresistible photo opportunity.

It is, however, with Hillary Clinton that we see the Medusa theme at its starkest

and nastiest. Predictably Trump's supporters produced a great number of images
showing her with snaky locks. But the
most horribly memorable of them adapted
Cellini's bronze, a much better fit than the
Caravaggio because it wasn't just a head: it
also included the heroic male adversary and
killer. All you needed to do was superimpose
Trump's face on that of Perseus, and give
Clinton's features to the severed head (in
the interests of taste, I guess, the mangled
body on which Perseus tramples in the
original was omitted). It is true that if you
crawl around some of the darker recesses
of the web, you can find some very unpleasant images of Obama, but they are very dark
recesses. It is also true that one satiric stunt
on US television featured a fake severed
head of Trump himself, but in that case the
(female) comedian concerned lost her job
as a consequence. By contrast, this scene
of Perseus-Trump brandishing the drip-
ping, oozing head of Medusa-Clinton was
very much part of the everyday, domestic

23. Caravaggio's head of Medusa has been replicated time and again to 'decapitate' female politicians. Here Angela Merkel and Hillary Clinton are given the Medusa treatment.

24. Uncomfortable souvenirs? Supporters of Donald Trump
in the US election of 2016 had plenty of classical images to
choose from. None was more striking than the image of
Trump as Perseus decapitating Hillary Clinton as Medusa.

American decorative world. You could buy it on T-shirts and tank tops, on coffee mugs, on laptop sleeves and tote bags (sometimes with the logo TRIUMPH, sometimes TRUMP). It may take a moment or two to take in that normalisation of gendered violence, but if you were ever doubtful about the extent to which the exclusion of women from power is culturally embedded or unsure of the continued strength of classical ways of formulating and justifying it – well, I give you Trump and Clinton, Perseus and Medusa, and rest my case.

OF COURSE, IT IS NOT quite enough to rest the case there without saying what we might actually do about this. What would it take to resituate women on the inside of power? Here, I think, we have to distinguish between an individual perspective and a more communal, general one. If we look at some of the women who have 'made it', we

*25. Margaret Thatcher 'handbags' one of her
ministers, the unfortunate Kenneth Baker.*

can see that the tactics and strategies behind their success do not merely come down to aping male idioms. One thing that many of these women share is a capacity to turn the symbols that usually disempower women to their own advantage. Margaret Thatcher seems to have done that with her handbags, so that eventually the most stereotypically female accessory became a verb of political power: as in 'to handbag'. And at an incomparably more junior level I did something similar when I went for my first interview for an academic job, in Thatcher's heyday as it happens. I bought a pair of blue tights specially for the occasion. It wasn't my usual fashion choice, but the logic was satisfying: 'If you interviewers are going to be thinking that I'm a right bluestocking, let me just show you that I *know* that's what you're thinking *and* that I got there first.'

As for Theresa May, it is even now too early to say, and there is an increasing possibility that we will one day look back to her as a woman who was put into – and kept in

– power in order to fail. (I'm trying very hard here not to compare her to Clytemnestra.) But I do sense that her 'shoe thing' and those kitten heels are one of the ways she shows that she is refusing to be packaged into the male template. She is also rather good, as Thatcher was, at exploiting the weak spots in the armoury of traditional Tory male power. The fact that she is not part of the clubbable boys' world, that she isn't 'one of the lads', has sometimes helped her carve out independent territory for herself. She has gained power and freedom out of the exclusion. And she is famously allergic to 'mansplaining'.

Many women could share perspectives and tricks like this. But the big issues that I have been trying to confront are not solved by tips on how to exploit the status quo. I don't think patience is the answer either, even though gradual change will almost certainly take place. In fact, given that women in this country have only had the vote for a hundred years, we should not forget to congratulate ourselves for the revolution that we have all, women and men, brought about. That said, if I am right about the deep cultural structures legitimating women's exclusion, gradualism is likely to take far too long – for me at least. We have to be more reflective about what power is, what it is for, and how it is measured. To put it another way, if women are not perceived to be fully within the structures of power, surely it is power that we need to redefine rather than women?

So far, in reflecting on power, I have followed the usual path in discussions of this kind, by focussing on national and international politics and politicians – to which we might add, for good measure, some of the standard line-up of CEOs, prominent journalists, television executives and so on. This offers a very narrow version of what power is, largely correlating it with public prestige (or in some cases public notoriety). It is very 'high end' in a very traditional sense, and bound up with the 'glass ceiling' image of power, which not only effectively positions women on the outside of power, but also imagines the female pioneer as the already successful superwoman with just a few last vestiges of male prejudice keeping her from the top. I don't think this model speaks to most women, who, even if they are not aiming to be president of the United States or a company boss, still rightly feel that they want a stake in power. And it certainly did not appeal in 2016 to sufficient numbers of American voters.

Even if we do restrict our sights to the upper echelons of national politics the question of how we judge women's success in that area is still tricky. There are plenty of league tables charting the proportion of women within national legislatures. At the very top comes Rwanda, where more than 60 per cent of the members of the legislature are women, while the UK is almost fifty places down, at roughly 30 per cent. Strikingly, the Saudi Arabian National Council has a higher proportion of women than the US Congress. It is hard not to lament some of these figures and applaud others, and a lot has rightly been made of the role of women in post-civil war Rwanda. But I do wonder if, in some places, the presence of large numbers of women in parliament means that parliament is where the power is *not*.

I also suspect that we are not being quite straight with ourselves about what we want women in parliaments *for*. A number of studies point to the role of women politicians in promoting legislation in women's interests (in childcare, for example, equal pay and domestic violence). A report from the Fawcett Society recently suggested a link between the 50/50 balance between women and men in the Welsh Assembly and the number of times 'women's issues' were raised there. I certainly do not want to complain about childcare and the rest getting a fair airing but I am not sure that such things should continue to be perceived as 'women's issues'; nor am I sure that these are the main reasons we want more women in parliaments. Those reasons are much more basic: it is flagrantly unjust to keep women out, by whatever unconscious means we do so; and we simply cannot afford to do without women's expertise, whether it is in technology, the economy or social care. If that means fewer men get into the legislature, as it must do – social change always has its losers as well as its winners – I am happy to look those men in the eye.

But this is still treating power as something elite, coupled to public prestige, to the individual charisma of so-called 'leadership', and often, though not always, to a degree of celebrity. It is also treating power very narrowly, as an object of possession that only the few – mostly men – can own or wield (that's exactly what's summed up by the image of Perseus or Trump, brandishing his sword). On those terms, women as a gender – not as some individuals – are by definition excluded from it. You cannot easily fit women into a structure that is already coded as male; you have to change the structure. That means thinking about power differently. It means decoupling it from public prestige. It means thinking collaboratively, about the power of followers not just of leaders. It means, above all, thinking about power as an attribute or even a verb ('to power'), not as a possession. What I have in mind is the ability to be effective, to make a difference in the world, and the right to be taken seriously, together as much as individually. It is power in that sense that many women feel they don't have – and that they want. Why the popular resonance of 'mansplaining' (despite the intense dislike of the term felt by many men)? It hits home for us because it points straight to what it feels like *not to be taken seriously*: a bit like when I get lectured on Roman history on Twitter.

So should we be optimistic about change when we think about what power is and what it can do, and women's engagement with it? Maybe, we should be a little. I'm struck, for example, that one of the most

26. There is no need for those who make a difference to have celebrity status. Few people know the names of the women founders of Black Lives Matter: Alicia Garza, Patrisse Cullors and Opal Tometi.

influential political movements of the last few years, Black Lives Matter, was founded by three women; few of us, I suspect, would recognise any of their names, but together they had the power to get things done in a different way.

But the picture overall is rather more gloomy. We have not got anywhere near subverting those foundational stories of power that serve to keep women out of it, and turning them to our own advantage, as Thatcher did with her handbag. Even I have been pedantically objecting to *Lysistrata* being played as if it were about girl power – though maybe that's exactly how we *should* now play it. And despite the well-known feminist attempts over the last fifty years or more to reclaim Medusa for female power ('Laughing *with* Medusa', as the title of one recent collection of essays put it) – not to mention the use of her as the Versace logo – it has made not a blind bit of difference to the way she has been used in attacks on female politicians.

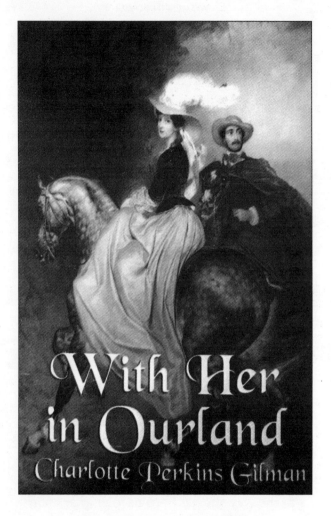

With Her in Ourland

Charlotte Perkins Gilman

27. *The cover of a recent edition of* With Her in
Ourland *hints at the way the women of Herland
could be tamed into a world of male power.*

The power of those traditional narratives is very nicely, though fatalistically, captured by Perkins Gilman. For there is a sequel to *Herland*, in which Vandyck decides to escort Terry back home to Ourland, taking with him his wife from Herland, Ellador: it's called *With Her in Ourland*. In truth, Ourland does not show itself off very well, not least because Ellador is introduced to it in the middle of World War One. And before long the couple, having ditched Terry, decide to go back to Herland. By now Van and Ellador are expecting a baby, and – you may have guessed it – the last words of this second novella are: 'In due time a son was born to us.' Perkins Gilman must have been well aware that there was no need for another sequel. Any reader in tune with the logic of the Western tradition would have been able to predict exactly who would be in charge of Herland in fifty years' time. That boy.

AFTERWORD

From lectures to book – and
the right to be wrong

TURNING LECTURES into permanent print can be a tricky business. How far do you stand back, re-think and polish the argument? How far do you try to keep the spirit, and maybe the rough edges, of the moment they were delivered? I have taken the opportunity of some very light updating. Barack Obama was still president when I gave the lecture that became Chapter 1 in 2014, and Theresa May's premiership looked in rather different shape when I gave the second lecture in March 2017 (and my casual aside about her being put into power 'in order to fail' – which *was* in the original version – could turn out to have been more prescient than I imagined). But I have resisted the temptation to make drastic changes, to introduce new themes or to develop at length some of the ideas that are merely floated here. I would like in the future to think harder about *how* exactly we might go about re-configuring those notions of 'power' that now exclude all but a very few women; and I would like to try to pull apart the very idea of 'leadership' (usually male) that is now assumed to be the key to successful institutions, from schools and universities to businesses and government. But that is for another day.

If you want to find more recent examples of the kind of abuse of women that I have been discussing, there is plenty more, easy to find, online. Trolls are not particularly imaginative or nuanced, and one Twitter storm tends to look much like any other. But just occasionally there are new angles, or at least revealing comparisons to be made. I was very struck during, and just after, the UK general election in the summer of 2017 by two disastrous radio interviews given by the Labour MP Diane Abbott and the Tory Boris Johnson. Abbott completely fell to pieces over the cost of her party's policy on police recruitment – at one point coming out with a figure that would have suggested that each new officer would have been paid about £8 a year. Johnson showed an equally embarrassing and stumbling ignorance on some of the new government's headline commitments; he didn't appear to have a clue on his party's policies on racial discrimination in the criminal justice system or on access to higher education. What caused these 'car crashes' is not the main point (Abbott was certainly unwell at the time). It was the different response, online and elsewhere, that was so striking.

It instantly became 'open season' on Abbott, ridiculed as a 'numpty', a 'fat idiot', 'bone-headed stupid' and much worse, with more than a sprinkling of racism thrown in (she is Britain's longest-serving black MP). Interpreted politely, the message was that she was simply not up to the job. Johnson came in for plenty of criticism too, but in a very different style. His interview was taken more as an example of laddish wayward-ness: he ought to get more of a grip, stop the bluster, concentrate and be a better master of his brief. Do better next time, in other words. The aim of Abbott's attackers (undermined, as it turned out, when she was re-elected with a vastly increased majority) was to make sure that she did not get a 'next time'.

Whatever your views on Abbott and Johnson, interestingly different kinds of double standards were on show here. It is not just that it is more difficult for women to succeed; they get treated much more harshly if ever they mess up. Think Hillary Clinton and those emails. If I were starting this book again from scratch, I would find more space to defend women's *right to be wrong*, at least occasionally.

I am not sure that I could find a classical parallel for that. Thankfully, not everything we do or think goes back directly or indi-rectly to the Greeks and Romans; and I often find myself insisting that there are no simple lessons for us in the history of the ancient world. We really didn't need the unfortunate Roman precedents in the region to know that modern Western military intervention in Afghanistan and Iraq might be a bad idea. The 'collapse' of the Roman Empire in the West has little to tell us about the ups-and-downs of modern geopolitics. That said, looking harder at Greece and Rome, helps us to look harder at ourselves, and to understand better how we have learned to think as we do.

There are many reasons for us still to pay attention to Homer's *Odyssey*, and it would be a cultural crime if we read it only to investigate the well-springs of Western misogyny; it is a poem that explores, among much else, the nature of civilisation and 'barbarity', of homecoming, fidelity and belonging. But for all that – as I hope this book shows – Telemachus' rebuke to his mother Penelope when she dares to open her mouth in public is one that is still, too often, being replayed in the twenty-first century.

From book to #MeToo – and reflections on rape

THE WORDS on the last few pages are those with which the first edition of this book was signed off and went to the printers. It was at the end of September 2017, before #MeToo had become the world's most famous hashtag, and when to most people the name 'Harvey Weinstein' still meant little more than a successful film producer. By the time *Women & Power* was published, issues of rape and sexual harassment were being discussed more publicly and intensely than we had ever known.

One year on, I am again signing off just days after the strong and moving testimony of Christine Blasey Ford to the Senate Judiciary Committee considering the nomination of Brett Kavanaugh to the US Supreme Court. As I write, we do not yet know whether Kavanaugh will in fact be nominated. And it is far too soon to be certain of the long-term impact of the Me Too movement more generally. I find myself torn between optimism and resigned pessimism. I certainly hope that people will one day look back to the autumn of 2017 as the moment that kick-started a social and sexual revolution. From the casting couch to the gropes behind the office photocopier, from New York to Nairobi, the spirit of Me Too may ensure that women are no longer silent about this kind of abuse. Just as important, it may also be a wake-up call for men – I mean, of course, for *some* men, for many are as horrified as most women at what has been alleged. It may represent a change of culture that stops them trying to trade favours for a bit of unsatisfactory sex; stops them pushing their tongues down unwilling throats; stops them treating sex as a perk of power.

But it may be more difficult than we imagine to convert a hashtag into practical action. In my gloomier moods, I fear that we may end up looking back to Me Too as the glorious herald of a change that never really happened, even if things never quite went back to what they were before. I do not only mean that we may be about to see a string of trials in which expensive defence lawyers ensure the acquittal of the guilty and not guilty alike. (I find it as hard as anyone to reconcile the absolute need for a fair and proper process in response to the various allegations with the knowledge that across the world the law has a blemished record in allowing rich men to get off.)

I also mean that, in some respects, the Me Too movement fits my arguments in this book uncomfortably well. As I have tried to show, right back to Philomela (who wove the denunciation of her rapist into her tapestry), women have often been allowed a limited voice, at least, in raising questions of their own treatment and abuse *as women*. #MeToo has made a gratifyingly loud noise that, for once, has been transmitted over most of the planet, but it still falls into that general category. Even more to the point, the root cause of the harassment that women have suffered (and the root cause of the earlier silence of so many) surely lies in the structures of power. If so, then the only effective remedy lies in a change to those structures. While fewer than ten per cent of the directors of the top Hollywood films are women (that was the case in 2017), men will remain the gate-keepers of success in the film industry, and the effect of women's voices on its sexual culture – however loudly those voices have now been raised – is likely to be limited.

Over the last twelve months, I have found myself celebrating the bravery of women who have spoken out. I have also inevitably found myself focussing more closely on issues of rape and consent – and how they relate to the themes of *Women & Power*, in particular narrative and story-telling. Through both chapters I have tried to show how important in defining, silencing or undermining women are the stories embedded for millennia in Western culture (whether the rebuke of Penelope by Telemachus or the beheading of Medusa); and I have tried to reveal the constraints on women constructing their own narrative of events (Philomela again, or Lavinia in Shakespeare's *Titus Andronicus*). In the light of Me Too, I have thought harder about the tales we tell ourselves about what has been done to us, or what we have done. How are those fleeting moments of human experience converted into the narratives that give them lasting significance, whether public, political or personal? I have not been able to resist going back to my own past, to the time I was raped, on a night train between Milan and Rome in 1978, and to the shifting ways in which that moment has taken its place in my own life story.

The bare bones of this incident are simple enough. I was a PhD student on my way to a few months' research in Italy, almost at the end of my journey, needing only to change trains late in the evening at Milan. I was very tired, encumbered with more luggage than I could easily manage on my own, but keen to practise my rudimentary Italian as I waited in the station bar for my connection.

I got talking to man who claimed to be an architect designing a biscuit factory outside Naples. Observing my exhaustion, he took my ticket and said that he would go and get me a couchette for the journey (I only had a 'sit-up' seat). Returning with the new ticket, he helped me and my cases and backpack to the train.

It was predictable in retrospect, but I wasn't awake enough at the time to spot his plan: what he had actually bought was a first class, two berth *wagon-lit* (then a particularly luxurious form of sleeping car). Once inside, he took my clothes off, had sex and retreated to the upper bunk. I woke up just outside Rome to find him on top of me again – before he handed me over to the steward, to be given a cup of coffee and deposited on the platform at Rome.

I had not screamed, run away or fought back during any of this. That is partly because I was too tired and saw no safety in sight, certainly not in the shape of the sleazy steward of the sleeping car, and I just wanted the whole business over. Besides, I had divided my precious thesis and notes into different cases (a misplaced confidence in the 'don't put all your eggs in one basket' principle) – which made any quick exit impossible, without the loss of months of work. I did not report it when I reached Rome because I had a shrewd, and I still suspect correct, sense that nothing whatsoever would come of it, particularly as I had no bruises to prove a fight. And I cannot claim that I was badly traumatised by the experience. I was lucky. Victims react differently. I have been left with no fear of Italian trains, late night stations nor – to share the joke that used to make me smile to myself – any aversion to Italian biscuits. But I was and remain angry. On no meaningful understanding of the term did I *consent* (the second time he did it I was asleep, for heaven's sake).

Some twenty years later I reflected back to this occasion in an essay in the *London Review of Books* – prompted by a new book arguing that sexual coercion should be understood through the lens of evolutionary biology (it's one way the male can maximise his chances of reproductive success ...!). My own experience certainly underpinned my critique of this particular argument, but I was also taking the chance to get a couple of decades of thoughts about what had happened to me into the open. I was particularly interested in the different ways that I had told and retold the story to myself and to others in the intervening period. One was to insist, as I have just done, that I had *been raped*, with all the powerlessness that the passive verb suggests. But I was equally capable of telling, and believing, some strikingly 'alternative' versions. As I put it in 2000:

> The first of these [was] the predictable slide from 'rape' to 'seduction': I wasn't overpowered or coerced; whatever happened in the station bar, it amounted to 'persuasion' or to an exercise of choice on my part. In fact, something like that was the first euphemistic version I chose

to tell my friends on arriving in Rome: I had, I complained, been 'picked up' in Milan and ended up in bed with the guy on the train; I never mentioned the word 'rape'. But I have also caught myself making sense of the whole incident as a much more emphatically willed part of my sexual history: the perfect degree-zero sexual encounter between complete strangers, happening in no single place but on the move, in the more or less exotic (or at least cinematically resonant) location of a wagon-lit. In this version, any seduction was done – however inadvertently – by me; the triumph was my own.

Almost another twenty years on, and in a very different sexual climate, I feel simultaneously proud and ashamed of those self-empowering narratives. The more I have now read about patterns of rape, the more I realise that 'biscuit factory man' was very likely indeed to have been a serial offender. Did I really think that his behaviour was a one-off piece of opportunism, still less a sudden *coup de foudre* at the sight of me? The practised exchange of my ticket and the eerily collusive relationship with the steward surely hint that this wasn't the first time, or probably the last, that he did this. But I have also started to wonder what kind of stories he told himself (or even perhaps his friends). Did he convert the whole seedy encounter, like I occasionally had, into a 'glamorous' zipless fuck? When he arrived in Naples later that morning, did he feel pleased with himself, slightly uncomfortable – or did he not stop to look back at it at all? Would he recognise *my* story, in which he appeared as a rapist?

I have similar questions about some of the behaviour reported over the last year in the context of Me Too. Assuming the allegations are true, I have wondered how these men explain *to themselves* what they have done. Suppose you had spent ten minutes in the morning forcing a woman into the bathroom of a hotel suite and assaulting her, how would you feel about yourself (let alone her) when you got back home? Some, no doubt, do stretch out with a gin and tonic, feeling little more than a balmy mixture of success and triumph. But my guess is that many more of them can barely bring themselves to reflect on their own sordid cruelty, except by reprocessing the encounter in their heads into a new and self-serving story: from some version of 'I couldn't help myself' to 'she was gagging for it', or even 'I've earned it'.

And that is why we must pay more attention to the narratives of the men now under accusation. I'm not for a minute suggesting that we should offer them a public platform for self-exculpation, to drown out the voice of the victims (there would be shades of Miss Triggs in that). I have no desire at all to let them off the hook. But unless we get to hear their version of events, we cannot possibly contest it, or expose the exploitation and corrosive hierarchies on which it is based. Power means many things in the world of Me Too. It certainly means empowering women to tell their stories fearlessly. But it also signifies our power to challenge, and to change, the stories that have offered these men their alibis – which many of them, let's face it, probably believe. Our aim is surely not just to bring the guilty to punishment, but – more important for the future – to ensure that such self-serving stories no longer seem plausible, even to those who tell them, to themselves.

Once and for all, 'she was *not* gagging for it'!

September 2018

REFERENCES AND
FURTHER READING

All the classical texts mentioned here are available in translation, in print and online. They can easily be tracked down in the Loeb Classical Library (Harvard University Press) and the Perseus Digital Library (http://www. perseus.tufts.edu/hopper/). Also useful are the up-to-date translations in 'Penguin Classics'.

Chapter 1

The put-down of Penelope is featured at Homer, *Odyssey* 1, 325–364. Aristophanes' 'hilarious' fantasy is *Ecclesiazousai* (*Assembly-women* or *Women in Power*). The story of Io is told in Ovid's *Metamorphoses* 1, 587–641; of

Echo in *Metamorphoses* 3, 339–508. Valerius Maximus is the Roman anthologist who discusses women speaking in public (at *Memorable Deeds and Sayings* 8, 3). The most famous version of Lucretia's speech is by Livy, *History of Rome* 1, 58. Philomela's story is told in *Metamorphoses* 6, 438–619. The second-century AD guru is Plutarch, who refers to women's voice in his *Advice to Bride and Groom* 31 (= *Moralia* 142d). For the old Roman slogan *vir bonus dicendi peritus*, see Quintilian, *Handbook on Oratory* 12, 1. Aristotle discusses the implications of the pitch of the voice in his *Generation of Animals* 5, 7 (786b–788b) and *Physiognomics* 2 (806b). The affliction of the community where the men speak like women is discussed by Dio Chrysostom, *Speech* 33, 38. For further discussion of gendered speech and silence in the classical world, see *Making Silence Speak: Women's Voices in Greek Literature and Society*, edited by A. P. M. H. Lardinois and Laura McClure, (Princeton, NJ, 2001) and Maud W. Gleason, *Making Men: Sophists and*

Self-Presentation in Ancient Rome (Princeton, NJ. 1995).

The authenticity of Elizabeth I's speech at Tilbury has been much disputed. Susan Frye, 'The Myth of Elizabeth at Tilbury', *Sixteenth-Century Journal* 23 (1992) 95–114, makes a good case for scepticism (and includes the standard text, for which see also http://www.bl.uk/learning/timeline/item102878.html). The life of Sojourner Truth is discussed by Nell Irvin Painter, *Sojourner Truth: a Life a Symbol* (New York, 1997); the variants of her speech are available online at http://wonderwombman.com/sojourner-truth-the-different-versions-of-aint-i-a-woman/. Henry James's essay on 'The Speech of American Women' is included in *Henry James on Culture: Collected Essays on Politics and the American Social Scene*, edited by Pierre A. Walker (Lincoln and London, 1999), 58–81. For the other quotations, see Richard Grant White, *Every-Day English* (Boston, 1881) 93, and William Dean Howells, 'Our Daily Speech', *Harper's Bazaar* 1906, 930–34, discussed by

Caroline Field Levander, *Voices of the Nation: Women and Public Speech in Nineteenth-Century American Literature and Culture* (Cambridge, 1998). Accurate estimates of the levels of online harassment are notoriously difficult, and there is the perennial problem of the relationship between actual and reported incidence; but a useful recent review with ample bibliography is Ruth Lewis and others, 'Online abuse of feminists as an emerging form of violence against women and girls', *British Journal of Criminology*, published online September 2016, https://academic. oup.com/bjc/article-lookup/doi/10.1093/bjc/ azw073

Fulvia's mutilation of Cicero's head is described by Cassius Dio, *Roman History* 47, 8, 4.

Chapter 2
The claim that Clytemnestra is *androboulon* is made explicit at Aeschylus, *Agamemnon* 11. Adrienne Mayor, *The Amazons: Lives and Legends of Warrior Women across the Ancient*

World (Princeton NJ, 2014) offers a closely argued alternative view of Amazons (but it does not convince me). The Greer translation of *Lysistrata* is G. Greer and P. Wilmott, *Lysistrata: the Sex-Strike* (London, 1972); *Looking at Lysistrata: Eight Essays and a New Version of Aristophanes' Provocative Comedy*, edited by David Stuttard (London, 2010) is a good introduction to the issues of the play. One classic ancient version of the Medusa story is Ovid, *Metamorphoses*, 4, 753–803. The leading attempts to reclaim the story of Medusa include: H. Cixous, 'The Laugh of the Medusa', *Signs* 1 (1976), 875–893, and *Laughing with Medusa*, edited by Vando Zajko and Miriam Leonard (Oxford, 2006). A useful collection of essays is *The Medusa Reader*, edited by Marjorie Garber and Nancy J. Vickers (New York and Abingdon, 2003). The views of the Fawcett Society on the Welsh Assembly are summarised in this online submission: https://humanrights.brightblue. org.uk/fawcett-society-written-evidence/ ('female legislators were responsible for raising childcare 62 per cent of the times it was debated, for raising domestic violence 74 per cent of the time, and equal pay 65 per cent of the time').

Afterword

Statistics on women in the film industry can be found Martha M Lauzen, 'The Celluloid Ceiling: Behind-the-Scenes Employment of Women on the Top 100, 250 and 500 Films of 2017', *The Celluloid Ceiling Report* 2018 (http://womenintvfilm.sdsu.edu). My account of my train journey from Milan to Rome is in the *London Review of Books*, 24 August 2000, 34–5.

ACKNOWLEDGEMENTS

IT WAS MY FRIEND Mary-Kay Wilmers, the editor of the *London Review of Books*, who first dreamed up the theme of the lectures that became the basis of this book, and who commissioned them for the *LRB* lecture series at the British Museum in 2014 and 2017. My thanks go to her, to the other staff of the *LRB*, and to the BBC who gave a version of what I said an airing on television and radio (for the record, the first lecture was the only one of my ventures onto television that the late A. A. Gill actually liked). Many other people have helped along the way to this publication. As always, Peter Stothard has generously shared his expertise (on this occasion, both of Classics and of contemporary politics); Caterina Turroni helped on the very final stages, and the very final words, when we were working together on an entirely different project; my family – Robin, Zoe and Raphael Cormack – patiently put up with hearing many trial versions of the lectures, for weeks on end (and Raphael first urged me to look at *Herland*); Debbie Whittaker was indispensable; and all the people at Profile, including Penny Daniel, Andrew Franklin and Valentina Zanca, have been as generous, efficient and patient as ever. I can't help recalling that, back in the early 1980s, Chloe Chard and I drafted an article on the topic of why women so rarely spoke up in university seminars; no one we sent it to wanted to publish it. Some of the arguments here must ultimately go back to conversations with Chloe.

But I owe most to Helen Morales, once my colleague in Classics at Newnham College, Cambridge, now Professor at the University of California, Santa Barbara. We talked through the issues, classical and otherwise, of women's power and voice over long transatlantic phone calls. Among many other things, she pointed me in the direction of the Medusa imagery. This book is for her.

LIST OF ILLUSTRATIONS

INDEX

Entries in *italic* refer to illustrations

A NOTE ON THE COVER

This is the original floor mosaic which
inspired the jacket to this volume.
Note the central Medusa figure.

The J. Paul Getty Museum, Malibu, California.
(Photo by VCG Wilson/Corbis via Getty Images)